IMPROVING STUDENT WRITING

A GUIDEBOOK FOR FACULTY IN ALL DISCIPLINES

by

ANDREW MOSS
CAROL HOLDER

given permission to photocopy pages to hand out

Department of English and Foreign Languages

California State Polytechnic University,
Pomona

KENDALL/HUNT PUBLISHING COMPANY
4050 Westmark Drive   Dubuque, Iowa 52002

Contents

Preface
To Faculty in All Disciplines

Our guidebook has two goals: to help you improve your students' writing and to show you ways of making your writing and reading assignments effective teaching tools. Our work with faculty in fields such as engineering, art history, biology, and political science has shown us how the use of basic techniques and ideas often improves students' writing significantly. We've also seen that when teachers clarify their assignments and sharpen their responses to their students' papers, the students learn more from their courses.

This guidebook offers practical methods and ideas to help you achieve these results. The first chapter explains methods of creating effective writing assignments, and the second chapter provides examples of assignments that have worked in various courses. In the third chapter we describe techniques of designing sound essay examinations, and our fourth chapter offers concrete strategies to help your students handle the writing process. Since writing assignments often require the reading of texts or articles, the fifth chapter outlines ideas for integrating writing and reading activities. The sixth and final chapter addresses the problems of evaluation, noting the approaches that have worked best for instructors teaching in a variety of disciplines. An inventory of techniques described in the guidebook appears in Appendix 3.

Much of the material in this guidebook comes from a research project we undertook in the summer of 1981 and from faculty seminars we conducted in 1980–82 at California State College, San Bernardino, and California State Polytechnic University, Pomona. Our goal in the seminars was to help faculty improve their writing assignments and their methods of evaluating students' papers. In the year following the seminars, we interviewed the faculty participants to find out the kinds of writing assignments and instructional techniques they developed as a result of their involvement in the project. A grant from the National Endowment for the Humanities supported the Cal State San Bernardino Writing Reinforcement Program, and our 1980 and 1981 seminars were part of that four-year project. The Cal Poly Pomona seminars were supported jointly by the University and by an Academic Program Improvement grant provided by the California State University Office of the Chancellor.

Our research project took us in the summer of 1981 to organizations and firms that hire Cal Poly graduates (e.g., the Bank of America, Hughes Aircraft Corporation, Burroughs Corporation). We interviewed professionals to find out the communications skills that our graduates need as they enter careers as managers, engineers, scientists, and planners. From our visits we learned that writing plays a vital role in all of these professions; we have included material from this research in Appendix 1.

As we wrote this guidebook, we realized how much our efforts were aided by the gracious help of many individuals. We are indebted to Linda Bunnell Jones, Harold Levitt, Jane Prather, and Paul Weller for their support of our projects at Cal Poly, and to Helene Koon for the opportunities and encouragement she gave us in our work at Cal State San Bernardino. We would also like to express our appreciation to the people who contributed to our research on writing in the professions: Leigh Branham, Gary Frederickson, Richard J. Champion, Thomas P. Cox, Mike Engel, Anthony J. Lumsden, Hob LeBlanc, Michael J. O'Sullivan, Kevin Quick, Bob Siggins, Jim Tracey, Bruce Waddington. To Debra Marler and Pat Kaae we extend our appreciation for helping us with our seminars and research projects—and for typing the guidebook manuscript. Ron Hill, Jenifer Underwood, and the staff of Cal Poly's Graphic Communications Services also deserve our thanks for their work in bringing the manuscript into published form.

Finally, we want to acknowledge the support and generosity of the people who made the guidebook possible: the Cal Poly Pomona and Cal State San Bernardino faculty who participated in our interdisciplinary writing seminars. To these faculty we extend our deepest gratitude; they broadened our understanding of their own disciplines and showed us the limitless resources of the creative teacher.

A. M.
C. H.

I
Assigning Writing

Whatever kinds of writing tasks you are at present assigning your students—research papers, essay exams, lab reports, book critiques, journals—your assignments are giving them a unique and valuable opportunity to learn. Through writing, students can learn to review and reflect upon the ideas they express, can learn to analyze concepts and see their relationships to one another. Unlike conversation, writing creates a visible record that one can ponder, add to, or revise. By challenging students to be analytical and reflective, well-conceived writing assignments deepen their understanding of any field, enabling them to create meaning out of raw data and express that meaning intelligibly to others.

Writing practice and well-designed writing assignments also prepare students for their careers. In our visits to organizations and firms in the southern California area, we came across many professionals who felt indebted to the college instructors who took writing seriously and who required it of their students. An executive in a computer firm told us that writing constitutes the backbone of software and hardware development, from the inception of a proposal through the creation of specifications and user manuals. Writing comprises a significant portion of his work, he told us, and he declared that the most useful experience he had in college was the writing of papers in a wide range of fields, from history to natural science. Another professional, a successful young architect in a growing planning firm, explained that the logical training he gained from one teacher who assigned writing was invaluable to him in the composition of environmental impact reports, land use studies, and planning proposals. At our visit to a research institute, biochemists told us that the instructors who required and evaluated their writing helped prepare them to write the grant proposals on which their research depends. We have provided further information about professional writing tasks in Appendix 1.

The conclusion is inescapable: college instructors are not only improving their students' learning experience when they carefully compose their writing assignments; they are also helping develop skills that the students will use to handle professional challenges throughout their lives.

Suggestions for Designing Effective Assignments

There are a number of ways to design effective writing assignments. The three ideas below have been particularly helpful to faculty in different fields:

1. Tie the assignment to your course objectives.

2. In your assignment handout, clearly specify the writing task, the audience, and the evaluative criteria.

3. Give students a chance to help one another.

Tying the assignment to your course objectives: Before you draft a writing assignment for your students, write a list of your course objectives (or review existing objectives), noting what you expect your students to learn from the course. Then design the assignment to help achieve one or more of those objectives. This approach to assignment design helps make the writing experience an excellent way for your students to master the course material (Herrington, 1981). It also helps ensure that the considerable time they spend writing their papers will be time well spent.

Here is how Cal Poly professor Ron Peterson had defined the objectives for his course, Introduction to Political Thought:

1. To expose the student to the elementary vocabulary and conceptions of political philosophy.
2. To give students experience in reading political philosophy.
3. To give students practice in analytical writing on subjects pertaining to political philosophy.

To achieve these objectives, Professor Peterson required his students to write four papers analyzing articles on political philosophy.

In each paper the students were to:

1. State the thesis of the article;
2. Identify the central argument and its main parts;
3. Describe the warrants or proofs that the author advanced in support of the thesis;
4. Show whether the argument was adequate to prove the thesis.

Specifying the writing task, the audience, and the evaluative criteria for your assignments: Clearly defining these three components of your writing assignments can give your students a sense of direction and result in better writing overall. Consider the task of the students who have to respond to this assignment:

> A twenty-page library research paper will be due the last day of classes this quarter. Review what you read thus far and select a topic that interests you.

A few students might view the assignment as an opportunity to pursue a topic of concern to them and would find a challenge in writing a paper that enabled them to explore their thoughts about it. Many students, however, would flounder in their attempt to fulfill the assignment. With few explicit directions, they would create diffuse, disorganized papers that would be burdens to read as well as to write. Too often the students would end up cutting and pasting ideas from other sources, evincing little or their own thought and point of view.

In contrast, note the clarity of the task in Peterson's assignment as well as in the six "Assignments That Work" in Chapter II. Note also that in several of the more complex assignments (e.g., the Agricultural Engineering and American Studies assignments, pp. 10–11) the instructor has broken up the overall task into several discrete steps, thereby helping students focus their efforts and organize their ideas.

2

An effective writing assignment also identifies the audience, or readers, of the paper. The intended audience of most assigned papers is usually the instructor. Yet addressing an instructor as the sole reader of a paper can often affect a student's writing for the worse. People who are lively, engaging, and interested in classroom discussion often become stilted or dull when communicating in written form to their instructors. Many of these students find it difficult to address a reader they believe knows more about the subject than they do. As a result they reach beyond their means for a style and vocabulary intended more to impress than to inform.

There are two solutions to this problem: creating an audience of peers or describing a fictional audience for the paper. When students know that their readers include their classmates, they're more likely to explain their ideas with the clarity and completeness non-experts require. There are a variety of ways to incorporate peer review in the classroom; one simple technique is to have students exchange final drafts and comment on them on the day they turn in the papers to you.

Creating a fictional audience for writing assignments can also be quite successful. An accounting assignment, for example, could require students to write a memorandum to a client. The writing of the memo would not only require the student to synthesize the course material and present it effectively; it would also reinforce an awareness that an accountant must be able to communicate clearly with clients. The fictional audience motivates students, for it helps them view the assignment as an activity that prepares them for future work. With the exception of the chemistry assignment, all of the examples in the "Assignments That Work" chapter specify fictional audiences.

You can also focus your students' efforts by letting them know in advance your criteria for evaluating their papers. Since your students know that you will evaluate their final products and assess what they have achieved, your statement of evaluative criteria can put them at ease and direct their energies toward that which is important. Your statement can also help you set your own objectives for marking the papers once the students have turned them in. Ron Peterson expressed the following criteria for evaluating his students' book critiques in political science:

1. The precise use of formal terms
2. An adequate development of paragraphs and their logical flow from one to another
3. Your grasp of the thesis and the structure of the author's argument
4. Correct grammar, diction, syntax, and spelling

Peterson included this statement of criteria on the assignment sheet itself; thus his students could better assess their own writing and understand the basis for his evaluation of their work.

Giving students a chance to help one another. You can structure writing assignments in such a way that students collaborate at different stages of the writing process while still producing their own written work. Doing so can

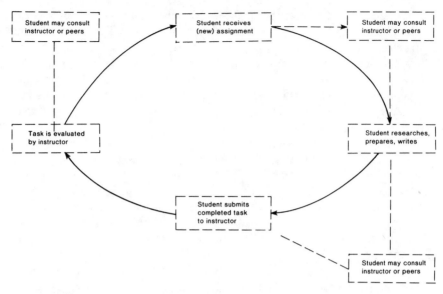

Figure 1. Cycle of a Student's Learning Activities—A Traditional Model

broaden the students' opportunities for learning and help you achieve your course objectives. Since teamwork is required in a wide variety of fields, collaborative writing efforts can also help prepare students professionally.

To illustrate the possibilities of group work, we have diagrammed two constrasting models of writing assignments. The traditional model (Fig. 1) represents the individual approach to written work; the student receives an assignment, writes the paper, submits it for evaluation, and does all of this with only the *possibility* of consultation with peers or instructor.

In the expanded model (Fig. 2), each of the four small circles represents an opportunity for group activity. The two top circles represent the small- and large-group discussions that can precede the writing of a draft; the two lower circles show the opportunities for group evaluation, either of the rough or final drafts of a paper.

How can these different activities help you to achieve your course objectives? If you want your students to practice analyzing a question and developing ideas, you can incorporate the group activities indicated at the top of the expanded model. If, on the other hand, you want to help your students improve the quality of their final drafts, you can use group activities to help them sharpen the language and tighten the development and organization of their papers. You can see the opportunities for such evaluation in the lower two circles of Figure 2; either the students can meet to review one another's rough drafts, or they can critique each other's final products just before turning them in to you.

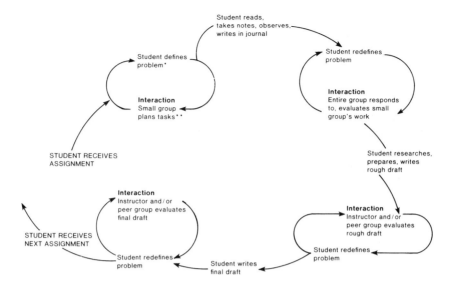

Figure 2. Cycle of a Student's Learning Activities—Expanded Model

The group evaluation need not take long, and the benefits can be substantial. Students can meet in groups of three or four, affixing a blank sheet to the top of their draft and passing it to the person next to them. All the members pass their papers at the same time, reading their neighbor's draft and making comments (you can suggest what to look for) on the readers' evaluation sheet. They don't take long to mark each paper, only a few minutes per essay, and they complete the process when the papers return to their original authors. The whole process can take place in 35–45 minutes.

One professor told us that the peer critiques had great value in her psychology class; she had the students reading articles throughout the quarter and writing critical analyses of them. Through the process of critiquing one another's final drafts, the students achieved a much stronger grasp of the material than they might have otherwise. As she explained, the less able students benefited by reading effective papers written by others; the abler students, on the other hand, clarified and sharpened their own understanding by explaining the course material to others.

Group processes offer another benefit to the students. Figure 2 shows how each group activity helps the students define and redefine their task and audience (the communications "problem"). By brainstorming with their peers

---

*Defining the problem involves identifying and handling all of the issues related to the development of a written product: audience, purpose, thesis, mode of discourse, choice of evidence and arguments, order of presentation, word choice, etc.

**e.g., debates, group presentations and reports.

they begin to understand potential interests and concerns of their audience; by reviewing one another's drafts they can raise questions not considered in earlier discussions.

You can tailor group processes to meet the specific objectives of your own classes. You may wish to use collaborative efforts only in the preliminary stages of the writing, when students are generating their ideas. Or you may find it more valuable to have students work together only after they have written a rough or final draft. The sample accounting assignment in Appendix 2 illustrates collaboration in both stages: generating ideas and evaluating drafts. You may want to experiment to find the combination that works best for you and your students.

Journals and Ungraded Writing

One of the most powerful tools to help you improve your students' writing may be one of the least understood: the journal. Journals are often used in many classes, particularly courses involving field work, such as social work or counseling. Students keep a log or journal of their experiences in the field and turn their journals in at the end of a term. We would like to extend the concept of student journals to include any collection of spontaneous, informal writings. The entries may include personal reactions and comments, but often they resemble rough or first drafts of more formal writing. This kind of writing is like "thinking on paper."

Journal writing can deepen students' understanding in any course. In journals, students can respond to readings, lectures, and other course activities. You can even use journal writing in class, having students make short journal entries at various points in a lecture or discussion. Unusual as this assignment may seem, it has been one of the most successful writing tasks assigned by faculty in a wide variety of fields, for it interrupts periods of listening and note-taking with an activity that allows students to reflect, make connections, or test their understanding (Fulwiler, 1979).

For example, you can stop a lecture at a critical point and ask your students to make a short journal entry (writing no more than five or ten minutes) in response to a question you pose. You can ask them to define a term, list examples, or explain in their own words something you have just demonstrated or discussed. In the act of writing, the students will have to demonstrate their understanding, even if only to themselves.

You can also begin a class session by having students make a journal entry about material covered in the previous class meeting or in the preceding night's readings. Starting a class with a brief writing assignment can improve continuity in your course as well as focus students' attention on the subject at hand. Finally, journal entries made at the end of class sessions give students a chance to summarize an important thing learned or write about something they don't yet understand. Though journal writing may seem to be an unorthodox kind of assignment if you have not used it before in your classes, remember that such personal writing forms the basis, the seedbed, of all the other kinds of writing: reports, critiques, essays. It is most helpful to assign, in addition to more traditional kinds of papers, the kind of writing that writers produce only for themselves.

As you assign journal writing of various kinds, we suggest that you observe only one rule: *Don't evaluate the journals.* The whole idea of expressive writing is that it must not be judged. You can require that students show you the journals periodically (collected and organized in a loose-leaf binder); you can then look them over and give credit to the students who turn them in. You can even write brief comments on the journal as a whole to encourage the writer, but to evaluate them is to defeat their purpose as vehicles of introspection and exploration. This is one writing assignment that is better left ungraded (much to the relief of many instructors).

Fine-Tuning

Whenever you experiment with a new idea or concept, there are bound to be unforeseen problems and difficulties; that is the nature of experimentation. When trying out new kinds of writing assignments or activities, you may encounter any one of a number of obstacles. The students' papers may not display the quality you had expected, or, if students are working in groups, a few may be shouldering all the work while others loaf. Some may even tell you that your writing assignments are inappropriate or too demanding and complain, "This is not an English class!"

We have discussed such difficulties with faculty in many disciplines. Some problems are inevitable. But the last thing one should do is discard a whole concept if only part of it does not work successfully. Some fine-tuning may often be needed when you introduce new procedures, new tasks. When you encounter difficulties, try to identify specific problems and make the necessary improvements or corrections. Were your instructions too vague even after refining them? Were you asking students to do too much in too short a time? Were the evaluative criteria still not clear enough? Often a colleague can identify the problem. You can also review the "Checklist for Evaluating Assignments" and the "Seventeen Suggestions for Making and Presenting Writing Assignments" below. In addition, feedback from your students (you'll need to sort out the usual workload complaints from genuine ideas about the problems) can help you revise your assignment.

Finally, keeping in mind your students' expanding levels of skill and knowledge, sequence your assignments from less to more complex and difficult tasks. Anne Herrington points out the importance of effective sequencing (Herrington, 1981); she mentions, for example, how one instructor started his students with short papers requiring definitions of basic terms, then moved to more complex assignments requiring the application of the terms to specific problems. This kind of sequencing helps students grapple with two tasks: the understanding of new vocabulary and course material, and the handling of often complex writing tasks.

7

SEVENTEEN SUGGESTIONS FOR MAKING
AND PRESENTING WRITING ASSIGNMENTS

Announcing the Assignment

1. Announce the due date of major writing assignments in the course syllabus.

2. Prepare a handout for each assignment and distribute it when you feel students should begin work on the paper.

3. In the handout, describe the topic and specify the type of paper you expect (e.g., report, term paper with certain format for documenting sources, essay, one paragraph), the due date, and the approximate length.

4. Break up a large assignment into smaller steps, especially if your students have had little experience with this type of writing.

5. Specify the audience for each assignment. Doing so will help the students make decisions about the development of ideas, the language of the paper, and matters of organization and paragraphing.

6. Provide students with information as to how the paper will be graded and to what extent the final course grade will reflect their performance on this assignment. Advise the students (preferably in the handout) that good writing will be rewarded and poor writing penalized—that organization, paragraphing, clarity of sentence structure and wording, spelling, punctuation, documentation format, etc., will affect the grade. If you have developed a system for grading papers, share it with the students when you distribute the assignment.

Improving the Assignment

7. Give the finished assignment to another to read to check for clarity in your instructions.

8. Occasionally do an assignment yourself. You may discover changes that need to be made, and, because you will have a clearer notion of the steps required in the completion of the assignment, you will be better able to break up the assignment into smaller steps or to advise the students on the *process* of doing the assignment.

9. Keep notes on the success and pitfalls of each assignment you develop and use. Such comments will help you modify the assignment the next time you want to use it. Save a good paper to distribute as a model in the future.

Types of Writing for Different Purposes

10. Experiment with different types of writing assignments suitable for your course. In addition to term papers and long reports, try assigning essays, critical summaries of assigned readings, letters, journals, and other short, more frequent, not necessarily graded writings. (Writing is most often used to *test* students' knowledge of a subject. Try instead to develop assignments that help students *learn* more about a subject.)

11. Use five-minute writings in class in place of multiple choice type quizzes to focus attention on concepts from readings or previous lectures.

12. Giving several shorter assignments, in or out of class, early in the quarter will allow you to identify students with serious problems and direct them to other courses or a tutoring center for help with their writing. Also, early writing assignments give all students an opportunity to benefit from your comments on and evaluation of their writing before they tackle a longer paper due toward the end of the quarter. Comments made on papers after final exams often go unread, unseen, and thus do not help the students write better on future assignments.

Presenting the Assignment to the Class

13. Take ten or fifteen minutes of class time to discuss the assignment and answer questions when you distribute the handout. Speak to problems the students can expect to encounter.

14. Early in the quarter or with each assignment, give the students a checklist to reinforce what you consider important in completing the assignment successfully. Another option would be to recommend a handbook, term paper manual, or other guide to writing in your department or discipline.

15. Students appreciate seeing a model of good writing of the type you will expect. Save papers from your students or set up a department file of model papers of various forms for this purpose.

16. After presenting the assignment, take some class time for small group activity to encourage discussion and generation of ideas for the paper. Also, students could present rough and final drafts to a small group for feedback from other students. Experiment with group writing exercises so that the weaker students have a chance to learn from the stronger students in a cooperative instead of competitive environment.

Collaboration of First-Class Minds

17. Find others in your department or school who also are trying to use writing more effectively in their courses. Share your experiences with writing assignments you have developed. Faculty who teach sections of the same course can pool ideas about using writing to help students learn more about the subject matter of the course.

CHECKLIST FOR EVALUATING ASSIGNMENTS

1. What is the purpose of the assignment?
2. Is the task clearly and succinctly described?
3. What verbal or conceptual abilities does the assignment ask the student to use or develop?
4. Does the assignment involve the whole communicating person (listening, speaking, reading, writing)? If not, could the assignment be revised to call all of these abilities into play?
5. Will the students have a clear idea of how their performance will be evaluated?
6. In what way does the assignment relate to preceding and ensuing course assignments in developing students' skills sequentially?
7. Can the assignment be revised to reflect more fully the course's aims in promoting the mastery of particular knowledge or the development of specific skills?

II
Assignments That Work

From faculty at Cal State San Bernardino and Cal Poly Pomona we have collected many successful assignments that show ways an instructor can develop stimulating and challenging writing tasks. We present six of them in this chapter with some or all of the following features (depending on information provided by the instructor):

1. **Task:** What the assignment asks the students to do.

2. **Audience:** The readers (fictitious or real) to whom the students are asked to address their papers.

3. **Process:** An explanation of the steps students are to take in completing the assignment.

4. **Evaluative Criteria:** The standards by which the instructor will evaluate the paper.

This list of features is adapted from a format developed by Anne J. Herrington (1981).

Assignment #1

Course: Introduction to Agricultural Engineering
Instructor: Ramesh Kumar, Cal Poly Pomona

In this introductory course, Professor Kumar wants his students to learn, among other things, what agricultural engineering is and what in particular Cal Poly's program offers. He has designed a writing assignment to help them meet these objectives. Also, he wants them to learn interview techniques, meet other professors in the department, become familiar with certain journals, and practice presenting technical information in non-technical terms. He has devised the following assignment to accomplish all of these objectives:

> One of the problems faced by high school seniors is to decide which school to go to and what major to choose. In deciding about this they read the information available about different majors and talk to persons already in those areas.
>
> Your assignment is to write an article (2–3 pages, double-spaced, typed) describing the discipline of agricultural engineering, career opportunities offered by this major, and the department at Cal Poly Pomona. The purpose of this article is to convince high school seniors to join the agricultural engineering field at Cal Poly Pomona.

In addition, Professor Kumar gives his students the following instructions to guide them in preparing their article:

1. Talk to all faculty members (there are only four of them here at this time) in the agricultural engineering department and find out the relevant information from them. When approaching the faculty you should have a list of questions with you.
2. Read the information brochure and Cal Poly catalogs.
3. Read the American Society of Agricultural Engineers publications for data about past activities and future plans of these professionals.
4. Make a list of ideas that influenced your decision to major in Agricultural Engineering at Cal Poly.
5. From the above resources develop an effective and persuasive article.

Kumar also presented with the assignment the following criteria that he would use to evaluate the students' papers:

1. Minimum use of technical terms
2. Easy to read and free of spelling and punctuation errors
3. Not more than three pages long
4. All references given proper credit
5. Originality; clear and convincing arguments

Assignment #2

Course: American Studies (Varieties of American Culture)
Instructor: Richard Johnson, Cal Poly Pomona

In this course, Professor Johnson wants his students to look beyond the surfaces of American cultural forms, to analyze and interpret what they find. Part of the course involves the study of gardens, and after visiting the Huntington Gardens in Pasadena (created and developed by the railroad baron Samuel P. Huntington), the students are to write an analysis of their experience. Professor Johnson structures the assignment so as to guide the students through a process of critical observation and analysis. Also, he defines for this paper a fictitious audience, a "group of octogenarians living in Breezier World," in order to help the students focus their writing. Here are Johnson's instructions verbatim:

> Write a 3–5 page interpretive essay on the Huntington Gardens as a cultural and multicultural interpretation of nature, based on the following:
> Audience: As one of the newly inaugurated docents of the Huntington Gardens, you have been given by your supervisor a letter written by a group of octogenarians living in Breezier World. In their letter they say that they recently took a Grayline tour to the Gardens, read the free brochure, and took the self-directed tour. "When we finished, we felt that we had missed something. Somehow there seemed to be a deeper meaning to the gardens than we had understood." They want to visit the gardens again, but they ask you first to explain what the gardens mean.

Pre-Writing Tasks:

(a) Visit the Cal Poly Rose Garden. Stay there for 5–10 minutes. In your journal, record exactly what you see, hear, and feel, including your own inner sensations. Do this before class on September 30, so that we might discuss it in class. The journal is for your eyes only.

(b) (In class) Understand the following major concepts or ideas:

(1) the changing relationships of man to nature (lecture);

(2) the particular American relationship to nature (film);

(3) the general function of gardens (discussion and audiocassette).

(c) Visit the Huntington Gardens. You may enjoy just walking through the gardens first, without attempting to analyze them. On your second walk, try to organize your observations around certain categories of analysis. I suggest:

(1) organizational structure and coherence;

(2) variety and contrast;

(3) effect upon you as a participant-observer.

(d) At the gardens, raise questions/problems which you want to answer/ solve but have been unable to. Examples: Why is the herb garden located where it is? Why is it organized functionally? What does that mode of organization imply about the main meaning which herbs have for humans? How does that meaning differ from the rose garden (at the Huntington), the cactus garden, etc.?

(e) Using the previous information, what can you infer about the relationship of Mr. Huntington to his gardens? Infer conclusions and show how these conclusions rest upon your previous observations.

(f) From all your observations, formulate a thesis, a single idea which can serve as a focal point for the entire paper. As you write your first draft, the thesis can be modified. The idea may come from major ideas presented in class (see b above).

Writing the Paper:

(a) State your thesis clearly, positively, and persuasively.

(b) Form coherent and persuasive analyses of data. Remember, your thesis is an abstraction. In the paper, be sure to support this idea with specific descriptions of characteristics of the gardens.

Evaluation: I will evaluate your essay with these criteria in mind:

(a) Were you a careful observer? Did you provide a clear and accurate description of what you saw?

(b) Were you able to organize your observations into meaningful categories?

(c) Were you able to understand the major ideas involved and relate your specific experience to those major ideas?

(d) Were you able to focus your curiosity into questions which could provide the next step for your additional learning experience (that is: "Here's what I discovered. Here's what I would like to understand more fully to make my learning experience deeper and more complete.")?

(e) Were you able to present your experience clearly and persuasively, supporting your conclusion with convincing evidence?

Assignment #3

Course: Cytogenetics
Instructor: David Campbell, Cal Poly Pomona

At the beginning of his course on cytogenetics, Professor Campbell is concerned about what his students remember from previous genetics courses; during the first week he wants them to review certain concepts that will be basic to his course. Instead of preparing a lecture on this material, Campbell asks his students to write a chapter on chromosome ultrastructure for a fictitious genetics textbook. He explains the task in this way, indicating the purpose and audience as he does so:

> You have been asked to help write a chapter on chromosome ultrastructure for a genetics text. The text is aimed at upper division biology majors. Your colleagues have asked you to prepare the introduction of this chapter, providing a review of the molecular structure of DNA. They have also asked that you continue on and review the histone proteins, as well as histone-histone interactions and the DNA-histone interactions which result in formation of the nucleosomes. Happily, they have agreed to take over the chapter with the topic of solenoid formation and higher degree of chromosome structure.
>
> The chaper material must be typed, double-spaced, on plain unlined paper. The format must be neat and consistent, suitable for a textbook. Your part is limited to five to ten pages by the publisher and should be at an even level of detail. Major sources of further detailed information are to be listed in a bibliography at the end of the chapter.

Evaluative criteria: Campbell states the following as the criteria on which he will evaluate the students' papers: accurate presentation of DNA structure; use of the correct molecules and terminology; a clear and logical sequence of developments leading to the higher orders of macromolecular assemblies; use of a consistent style and format appropriate for text material.

Assignment #4

Course: Organic Chemistry
Instructor: Philip Beauchamp, Cal Poly Pomona

Professor Beauchamp requires students in this lower-division chemistry course to keep a journal. Each week's journal entry is an informal paper on an organic substance in their lives (chemicals found in foods, cosmetics, medicines, soaps, etc.). This assignment allows the students to explore the relevance of chemistry to their daily lives as well as to practice writing and to learn the use of reference materials. Here is how Beauchamp presents the task to his students:

> **Journal Writes:** The journal write will help make you aware of how intimately organic substances are involved in our daily lives. Each week I would like you to find one organic substance used in your daily environment and see what you can discover about its uses and effects on you and/or the environment.

These substances can come from the food you eat, the medicines you take, cosmetics you use, shampoos, soaps, detergents, pesticides in the environment (Malathion), or any other substances you might come across in the news, newspapers, or magazines. The journal write should include:

(1) your name

(2) common name of substance

(3) formal name of substance

(4) structural formula

(5) source of substance (i.e. commercial product)

(6) paragraph on feelings, including

    (a) what the functions are

    (b) what side effects are present

    (c) what you found interesting

    (d) your thoughts on its use

(7) reference(s) which you used

The journal write will be due at the beginning of the period each Friday. It will be accepted up to one week late with a reduction of one grade.

Professor Beauchamp also gave his students the following journal entry which he wrote to make the assignment clear:

Sample Journal Write

Substance: Common Name: Benzoyl Peroxide
              Chemical Name: Benzoyl Peroxide

Structure

$$C_6H_5 - \overset{\text{O}}{\overset{\|}{C}} - O - O - \overset{\text{O}}{\overset{\|}{C}} - C_6H_5$$

or

$$C_6H_5 - \overset{\text{O}}{\overset{\|}{C}} - O - O - \overset{\text{O}}{\overset{\|}{C}} - C_6H_5$$

Source
I noticed this substance while watching a T.V. commercial for BufOxal, a face medicine in which benzoyl peroxide is the active ingredient.

Journal Write #1
This compound was reported to be used as a catalyst for hardening certain fiberglass resins. Rats can consume 950mg/kg body weight (poor rats) without fatalities, though death was reported with doses of 250mg/kg if given to rats intraperitoneally (just inside the membrane which lines the cavity of the abdomen). This is a moderately toxic compound and I don't feel that I would want to use this substance over a long period of time, though short time use appears safe enough.

14

References

1. *Clinical Toxicology of Commercial Products,* Section II, p. 22.

2. The structure was given in the *Handbook of Chemistry and Physics,* Section C, p. 196.

Assignment #5

Course: Counseling Practicum
Instructor: David Lutz, Cal State San Bernardino

Professor Lutz's course is designed to prepare his graduate students for work as counselors. Here are the course objectives as Lutz defines them:

1. Develop basic counseling skills.

2. Develop as professionals, especially in terms of behavior with clients and professional responsibility.

3. Develop the ability to communicate your impressions about a client, both orally and through the written word.

4. Learn case management techniques including process notes and record keeping.

To help his students achieve these objectives, particularly the third and fourth, Lutz has them write case reports which he evaluates. His own description of the assignment is as follows:

> In the agencies in which you will be working certain paper work is required. One example of this paper work is what is often called a case report. This assignment is designed to have you write a case report concerning one of your clients. Your case report should give the reader a concise summary of your interactions with your client in therapy.
>
> Audience: A case report typically has three potential readers. First, it may be utilized by another therapist who takes on this client at some later date. It is important that this therapist knows what has happened in therapy with you to evaluate if the problem differs in any way. Secondly, it may be used as the basis of a report to another agency that the client may utilize. While the case report itself will not be sent, it may be summarized in the letter to that agency. Third, and most important from a legal standpoint, your records including the case report may be subpoenaed by a court at some later date. Remember that it is the client's right of privilege, not the therapist's. Don't put anything in your case report that you would not be willing to say in court. Thus, be sure to discriminate between your own thoughts and ideas and the client's.

Requirements:

1. A brief description of the presenting problem.

2. The course of therapy. How did therapy progress from your first session to this point?

3. Your reactions to your client and the therapeutic process. How did you feel about therapy with this client? Was it threatening, boring, exciting? Did it move slowly, quickly?

4. What are your hypotheses about the future for this client?

This paper should be no longer than four, typed, double-spaced pages.

Evaluative Criteria: The report will be evaluated with the following points in mind: (1) Does your report provide a clear conception of the client? This includes not only the problem itself but how the client presented him/herself in therapy. (2) If I were the next therapist with this client, would I have some idea what to try next and what to avoid with this client? (3) Does the report do more than simply state what happened in the first session, second session, etc.? Summarize and conceptualize.

Assignment #6

Course: Criminal Justice Administration: Court Administration
Instructor: Frances Coles, Cal State San Bernardino

In her course Professor Coles seeks to achieve three objectives: a) to familiarize her students with courtroom processes, b) to help them identify problem areas in the court's administration, and c) to help them develop solutions to these problems. The writing task she created helps to meet all three objectives. Here is her description of the assignment:

As a candidate for judicial office you are speaking to members of a local professional club, most of whom have a passing knowledge of courtroom processes. Describe two reforms you would initiate to reduce courtroom delays at a trial. Explain how each measure will achieve that purpose. Also explain potential side effects, either beneficial or detrimental, to the courtroom process. You are speaking to the professional club in an effort to secure their endorsement of your campaign.

Requirements: In order to write the assignment you must (1) be familiar with book and lecture material on the subject of courtroom trial procedure; (2) be familiar with the issue of delays in court; (3) be able to integrate any proposed solutions you are familiar with into the context of the question.

Evaluative Criteria: Your instructor will evaluate your essay with these criteria in mind: (1) Did you clearly understand the issue addressed? (2) Did you clearly state the reforms you suggested? (3) Did you present the potential side effects in an effective and logical manner? (4) Did you state the ways in which your suggested reform would alleviate courtroom delays?

III

Essay Examinations

A good essay examination allows the students not only to demonstrate what they have learned but also to connect ideas or approach the course material in new ways. Thus, in these special writing assignments, you can test your students' understanding and also give them an opportunity to use writing as a tool of synthesis and discovery. But to do so (and to make your job correcting the exams easier) you must design the questions carefully. Consider, for example, the following essay exam questions:

What are some aspects of American society that encourage rape?

Discuss developments in the English novel in the Victorian period.

Neither of these questions does much to direct students or help them organize their knowledge. The phrasing of the psychology question is ambiguous because of the vague words *aspects, society,* and *encourage.* The literature question is just too broad and invites the students to participate in a writing marathon. The instructors who gave these questions received a large number of poorly focused papers and encountered some difficulty evaluating them and responding to them.

Another kind of question that does not result in a satisfactory essay-writing experience is the objective question masquerading as an essay question. Questions such as "What are the five components of . . . ?"—questions that do not require complete sentences in response—are not essay examination questions, even if students write their answers in sentence form. (When scoring the responses to questions like these, the instructors look for the five components, four examples, etc. . . .)

Essay questions usually require more than recall of factual material. The following list, "Important Word Meanings," developed by the UCLA History Department and distributed to students in the UCLA Learning Skills Center, suggests the kinds of questions more suited to an essay (or paragraph) response.

Important Word Meanings

Good answers to essay questions depend in part upon a clear understanding of the meanings of the important directive words. These are the words like *explain, compare, contrast,* and *justify,* which indicate the way in which the material is to be presented. Background knowledge of the subject matter is essential. But mere evidence of this knowledge is not enough. If you are asked to *compare* the British and American secondary school systems, you will get little or no credit if you merely *describe* them. If you are asked to *criticize* the present electoral system, you are not answering the question if you merely *explain* how it operates. A paper is satisfactory only if it answers directly the question that was asked.

The words that follow are frequently used in essay examinations:

1. **summarize** sum up; give the main points briefly. *Summarize the ways in which man preserves food.*

2. **evaluate** give the good points and the bad ones; appraise; give an opinion regarding the value of; talk over the advantages and limitations. *Evaluate the contributions of teaching machines.*

3. **contrast** bring out the points of difference. *Contrast the novels of Jane Austen and William Makepeace Thackeray.*

4. **explain** make clear; interpret; make plain; tell "how" to do; tell the meaning of. *Explain how man can, at times, trigger a full-scale rainstorm.*

5. **describe** give an account of; tell about; give a word picture of. *Describe the Pyramids of Giza.*

6. **define** give the meaning of a word or concept; place it in the class to which it belongs and set it off from other items in the same class. *Define the term "archetype".*

7. **compare** bring out points of similarity and points of difference. *Compare the legislative branches of the state government and the national government.*

8. **discuss** talk over; consider from various points of view; present the different sides of. *Discuss the use of pesticides in controlling mosquitoes.*

9. **criticize** state your opinion of the correctness or merits of an item or issue; criticism may approve or disapprove. *Criticize the increasing use of alcohol.*

10. **justify** show good reasons for; give your evidence; present facts to support your position. *Justify the American entry into World War II.*

11. **trace** follow the course of; follow the trail of; give a description of progress. *Trace the development of television in school instruction.*

12. **interpret** make plain; give the meaning of; give your thinking about; translate. *Interpret the poetic line, "The sound of a cobweb snapping is the noise of my life."*

13. **prove** establish the truth of something by giving factual evidence or logical reasons. *Prove that in a full-employment economy, a society can get more of one product only by giving up another product.*

14. **illustrate** use a word picture, a diagram, a chart, or a concrete example to clarify a point. *Illustrate the use of catapults in the amphibious warfare of Alexander.*

Writing the Questions

As with any other writing, you can expect to write several drafts of the essay questions you are developing for an examination. Because you do not want students to use exam time trying to figure out what you want them to do, avoid ambiguous terms or conflicting instructions. Many instructors have found that students write better exams in response to clearly focused questions, those that describe the tasks briefly and even indicate the readers or audience to whom the students are to address their answers. Cal State San Bernardino professor Robert Blackey found limitations in this traditional question:

> Present and evaluate the argument for the position and action of Mary, Queen of Scots (or the Puritans).

He found he could test his students' understanding of the same material and at the same time stimulate more interest in the topic with the following revision of that traditional question:

> Answer either A or B (30 minutes):
> Imagine you are an attorney for the defense. You have presented your case and you are now writing your summation to the jury in order to support the case of . . .
>
> A. Mary, Queen of Scots, or
>
> B. The Puritans in the reign of James I.
>   Trace the history of the people involved, justify their cause, and thrash their opponents. (It's a matter of life or death.)

Professor Blackey has described the task, specified a context and audience for the writing, and simultaneously encouraged the students to write with imagination as well as awareness of this historical conflict.

Another question he developed involved a letter format:

> Imagine you are a Puritan (you decide the denomination) living in London in the mid-1650's. Using your knowledge of social, religious, economic, and political history, describe and evaluate the world you see around you (i.e., what it was like and how it has changed) in a letter to a fellow Puritan who emigrated to America. In addition to using your imagination, you should fill your letter with real, concrete, and factual material to render it valid.

Having students write to alternative audiences can be effective on essay exams in many disciplines. Here's a question developed by Cal Poly professor Ramesh Kumar for students in an Agricultural Engineering class:

> Your employer has just bought a sprayer which has an engine to drive a piston pump and a twenty-foot wide boom. There are no nozzles on the boom. Your employer wants you to tell him, in a one-page memo, how he should go about deciding which nozzles to buy for his sprayer. Your job is to describe various conditions (make up one or two) under which this sprayer will be used and describe the procedure for nozzle selection. Your employer does not understand much math, so do not include any calculations. Remember your job could depend upon the clarity and effectiveness of this memo.

Professor Kumar indicated in this question what the students were to do in their responses and further specified and described a particular reader and a particular format for the answers. With this question, he has simulated a writing task the students could expect to face as professionals and also established a need for clarity and conciseness in the responses.

Whether you use the more traditional type of question or one like Kumar's or Blackey's with audience and context defined, you will want to test and revise the question itself for clarity. We have several suggestions for doing so:

1. Give your question to a colleague or a friend (preferably someone in a different discipline) and see if that person has any difficulty understanding your instructions. (You could, for example, ask your friend to paraphrase your question.)

2. Write a response to your own question. In the process of writing the essay you'll be asking your students to write, you may discover problems with the question and see ways of improving the question or your instructions.

3. When you evaluate your students' essays, look for recurring difficulties and see if they could be related to a problem with the question itself. If they are, rewrite the question to avoid that difficulty with the same question on a future exam.

Here is a checklist you can use to evaluate the questions you develop:

Checklist for Evaluating Essay Examination Questions

1. Is the question phrased clearly and specifically?
2. What knowledge is the question intended to elicit?
3. What writing skills does the question require of the student?
4. Does the question clearly specify the mode of development required (e.g., comparison, description, evaluation)?
5. Is the student given adequate time in which to answer the question?
6. Did the course adequately prepare the student to answer the question?
7. Is the basis for evaluating the student's response clearly specified?
8. In what ways is responding to this question a learning experience for the student?
9. What relationships, if any, exist between the examination as a written assignment and the other written assignments in the course?

Indicating Evaluation Criteria

Students appreciate knowing the criteria you will use to evaluate their writing in essay examinations. You need not make extensive comments about standards. A short statement at the bottom of the exam will do:

Each essay is worth 9 points:
3 for demonstrating your understanding of key concepts;
3 for details and facts used to support general statements;
3 for clarity and organization of the essay.

Ramesh Kumar attached to his essay question on the choice of nozzles the following criteria:

1. Your essay should be easy to read and free of spelling and punctuation errors.
2. It should not be more than 1 1/2 pages long (250–400 words).
3. It should describe the total procedure without the use of math.

Some Final Considerations: Helping Your Students Write Better Exams

Examination essay writing—writing within a limited time period—gives students practice writing under pressure, creating a first draft that communicates clearly, though it may not have the polish of revised and edited prose. You may find it necessary, however, to instruct students on writing essay exams. Here are some reminders you can give students the class meeting before the examination:

Instructions to Students on Writing Essay Exams

1. Read the entire test before you start writing. If there are several questions or parts of the exam, budget your time, saving five or ten minutes for proofreading at the end of the exam period. (Bring a watch to the examination if a clock is not visible.) It is better to write something on all questions than to omit a question because you have devoted too much time to other parts of the test.
2. Follow directions carefully, underlining key words in the instructions. If you are to answer A or B, for example, underline the *or* and don't answer both. Not reading directions carefully is one of the major causes of poor performance on exams.
3. Plan before you write. Your essay should start with a thesis sentence that answers the question directly, that shows the conclusion you have come to after thinking about the question. Jot down (on the examination or other scratch paper) a brief outline of the major points you will use to support your thesis.
4. Write the essay, following your outline. Though your essay should be factual (not just opinions and generalizations), you will not have enough time to write all the details you know. Therefore, you must be selective. Choose those facts, details, examples, or other points that will *best* support your thesis.
5. Keep your thesis in mind as you write. Time is short so don't allow yourself to be distracted by a side issue. Everything you include should be pertinent to answering the question and supporting your thesis.
6. Check the time occasionally. Conclude your essay and go on to the next question when the time you have budgeted has passed. Leave some space to write more in case you have time later to go back to a question that you couldn't finish.
7. Proofread your essays at the end of the exam period. It's easy to misspell even simple words, to omit letters or words, or to transpose numbers 1952 for 1592) when you are writing under pressure. Make any corrections or additions neatly. Although unity, organization, and development are most important to clear communication in an essay examination, correct as many errors in spelling, punctuation, and grammar as you can before you turn in your test.

IV

Strategies for Helping Students

What can you do when a clear and thought-provoking assignment still results in poorly written papers? How can you help students who misread your question or misunderstand major vocabulary terms? What do you tell students who pour information into their papers but who can't analyze or integrate it?

Your written comments on the papers can point out weaknesses and show a pathway to improvement; in Chapter VI we'll discuss some ways to communicate effectively when you mark papers. But you also have another strategy that can help students overcome their writing problems. Often a flawed paper results from a snag in the process that created it. Some students delay writing until the last minute, then dash off a draft that reveals its haphazard creation in every sentence. Others have difficulty getting their ideas on paper; their work is often thinly developed as a result. Still others proceed methodically enough, but their efforts involve little more than the cutting and pasting of others' ideas; they have problems integrating material and showing relationships among ideas.

To help these students, you can show them that writing usually involves a series of distinct stages, each of which requires different kinds of mental activities. These stages include the following:

1. Analyzing the assignment

2. Brainstorming

3. Gathering information (if the assignment calls for research)

4. Planning

5. Drafting and revising

6. Proofreading

Analyzing the Assignment

For many students, to whom the writing process involves only an outline and a final draft, these stages may require some explanation on your part. When you first hand out an assignment, for example, you can encourage students to analyze the task required of them and to identify the audience (particularly if you have created a fictitious audience). Urge them to underline such key directional words as *compare, trace,* or *evaluate;* you may even wish to duplicate and hand out the list of Important Word Meanings on pages 17 and 18. Students can perform this analysis in small groups (see pp. 3–6), or they may wish to do it in their journals (see pp. 6–7). Note how one student used a journal entry to analyze both the task and the audience in the freshman writing assignment that follows.

The Dormitory Television Dilemma

Background: The dormitory in which you live has had an old color television set in its lounge for many years, a set that has provided news and entertainment to all the dorm students. It is the only set in the building. Recently it broke down completely; its failure put it beyond the scope of reasonable repair, and so a faction of students is clamoring to buy a brand new set (a proposition that will cost the dorm residents a few hundred dollars). Another group opposes the purchase of a T.V.; they believe that the money could be better applied to other purposes: new books for the dorm library, repairs to the volleyball court, etc. In response to both the positive and negative feelings about the purchase of a new set, the Dorm Council has decided to call for a meeting in which the two factions will debate the merits of such a purchase.

Task: Your task will be to write a position paper which one member of your group can read aloud at the beginning of the debate. The paper (500–750 words) will articulate the basic outline of your argument either for or against the purchase of the television set.

The student who wrote the following journal entry was on the team favoring the purchase of a new television:

The Entry

The problem is to convince the dorm board that the TV's benefits outweigh the drawbacks. We'll have to list the benefits, of course, but we should also talk about some liabilities—we can answer those. I guess the Board is neutral about this—at least they should be. What kinds of arguments would work? If the other side is going to say that the money would be wasted on a TV, maybe we could answer with an educational argument—TV's values in news, specials, etc. Some specifics could be helpful. . . .

This journal entry helped the student to begin thinking about his task and his audience. Completing this important step of analysis helped direct the student, helped focus the writing process from the very beginning. Students who go astray in their papers often do so at the very start, jumping into the writing without a careful consideration of the task before them.

Brainstorming, Research, and Planning

Even after they have analyzed an assignment capably, some students will still have difficulty generating ideas, particularly on extended reports and papers. As a result, the work they turn in is often poorly developed. One suggestion you can make to such students is to use a common brainstorming technique of jotting down all the ideas that come to mind about the subject at hand, never stopping to formulate sentences or to delete irrelevant material. The writer must keep jotting, never judging what he or she comes up with. Many studies show that creative people can be playful with ideas, can suspend their critical faculties when they embark on new projects (Flower and Hayes, 1977). Students can learn to do the same as they begin a paper or report; the results will be richer, the process more rewarding.

We have listed the step of information gathering after brainstorming because writers often recite their existing knowledge and ideas about a subject before seeking new material. Many times writers will also brainstorm ideas after they have researched a topic; the steps need not follow one another in a rigid sequence.

The planning stage is critical to the quality of the final draft; it is during the planning phase that the writer begins to organize the material and arrange it according to concepts and categories. Even though many students outline their ideas, their papers are often as disorganized as those written without an outline. One of the disadvantages of traditional outlines (i.e., those using a sequence of Roman numerals and indented letters and numbers) as a planning device is that they constrict the process of generating ideas, particularly at a stage when the writer still needs to experiment with the material. Flower and Hayes, on the other hand, have described the advantages of tree-diagramming. Not only does the method clarify relationships by portraying them visually; it also gives writers considerable flexibility to alter their ideas or their format even while in the drafting stage. Below you see how one student brainstormed ideas in response to the dormitory television assignment; following that is his tree diagram of the material. Although the assignment did not require formal research, the techniques used by the writer apply to longer, more complex assignments.

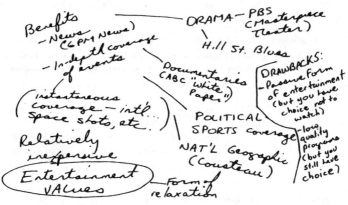

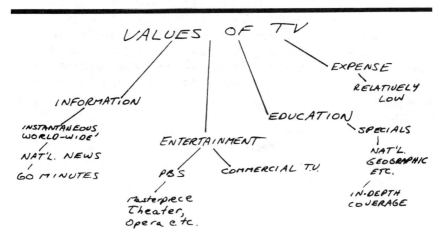

Drafting and Revising

Some of your students may have little difficulty analyzing the assignment, gathering information, generating ideas, or organizing those ideas into a coherent outline. Yet they may still be turning in flawed or inadequately developed papers; sometimes they may be turning them in late or not at all. Often the problem lies at the next stage of the writing process: drafting. Ask your students if effective writers are those who can produce a high-quality draft on the first try. You may be surprised to discover how many students cling to this myth. When told that F. Scott Fitzgerald labored over successive drafts of his novels, one student replied, "Well, he mustn't have been a very good writer!" Unaware that revision plays such an important role, many students are inhibited by the image of the Perfect First Draft. They write a sentence and ponder its correctness, write another and ponder anew. Their fluency crippled, they labor mightily and produce little.

Yet autobiographical material and interviews with professional writers have demonstrated the iterative process of writing: the process of reshaping language to explore and express an idea. The economist John Kenneth Galbraith, a respected literary craftsman, has remarked about how it takes five drafts to complete a manuscript, four drafts when he's able to be "spontaneous."

To these students you can suggest a simple distinction: the writer as talker versus the writer as critic. Encourage the student to "talk out" the first draft on paper, not worrying about the niceties of its structure, its development, or its mechanics. While "talking" on paper, the writer can keep in mind the image of the reader, whether that reader is you, a fellow student, or a fictitious person described in the assignment. The important thing is to get the whole draft out. When the first draft is completed, the "writer as critic" enters the scene.

We have used the term *drafting* to indicate the complete rewriting of a paper and *revising* to mean the rewriting or rearrangement of parts of it. Sometimes students may write two or more complete drafts in response to a particular assignment; sometimes they may be revising only a portion of a draft. The extent of alteration depends on the nature of the assignment and the time available to the students. Whatever the case, it is important to realize that a writer will be alternating between the roles of writer as talker and writer as critic. It is also useful to realize that a writer may need to go back, to return to earlier stages of the process even after finishing a draft. There may be an additional need to brainstorm, to plan, or even to re-analyze the assignment itself.

Criteria for Revision

What guides can you give students to help them revise? You might hand out a copy of the scoring guide you use (see pp. 43–45), or you can distribute a checklist such as the following:

A Writer's Checklist

1. **The Thesis:** Can you underline it? Is it expressed clearly and specifically?
2. **The Paragraphs:** Do they each develop one main idea? Do they develop the ideas adequately and coherently?
3. **Evidence:** Are your examples sufficient to support your ideas?
4. **Definition:** Have you identified the key terms in your paper and defined them adequately?
5. **Sentences:** Do the sentences express your main ideas concisely and effectively?
6. **Transitions:** Do the transitions work well to tie one part of the paper to another?
7. **Word Choice:** Do the words you use in the paper aptly and precisely express your meaning? Have you used specialized or technical words correctly?
8. **Errors of Structure and Usage:** Can you spot any major errors (e.g. fragments, run-on sentences, agreement errors) particularly the problems that have appeared most frequently in your own writing?
9. **Audience:** In your own judgment, does the writing as a whole make the most effective appeal that it can to the audience for which it is intended?

A useful guide for stylistic revision is Richard Lanham's "paramedic method," a simple formula for eliminating unnecessary verbiage (Lanham, 1979). By taking such steps as discarding superfluous prepositions and tightening the syntax, a writer using the method can turn prose such as this:

> The principal reason for their creation of the clinic was the inadequacy of the health care in the community.

into this:

> They created the clinic mainly because the community lacked adequate health care.

Once a writer has revised a paper to his or her satisfaction, proofreading for spelling, grammatical, and typographical errors is the last and essential step. You can motivate students to carry out this step by indicating that the paper's correctness will also figure in the final evaluation.

V
Integrating Reading and Writing

There are several reasons for integrating your reading and writing assignments. First of all, the two processes are already connected in any course. The students who are reading assigned text material throughout a term will know how much they have assimilated and understood only when faced with the challenge of explaining it in an essay test or take-home writing project. Conversely, the paper or report they write will require the synthesis of material from course readings or reference materials; in order to write a successful paper they must have understood what they read.

In addition there is now considerable evidence to show that writing actually helps to increase a person's comprehension of what is read. Researchers (Grobe and Grobe, 1977; Lunsford, 1978) have found correlations between the levels of students' reading and writing skills, but there is more specific evidence for a positive relationship in the nature of comprehension itself. Smith (1978) and others have defined comprehension as the process of relating new information to the stock of knowledge one already possesses. Readance, Bean, and Baldwin (1981, pp. 41–45) have described the process in terms of three levels of comprehension: text-explicit, text-implicit, and experiential. On all three levels the writing process can help to strengthen a person's understanding of a text.

How does this happen? The *text-explicit* level involves an understanding of the material on a purely factual, or recall, basis. A text-explicit question about Martin Luther King's "Letter from Birmingham Jail" might be as follows:

> What reasons does King give for following a course of nonviolent civil disobedience in Birmingham, Alabama?

This question asks the reader to supply information provided by King in his letter. The reader needs to do no critical thinking—only to find and restate the reasons for Dr. King's course of action.

A *text-implicit* understanding, on the other hand, involves an ability to infer meanings not explicitly stated in the text. A text-implicit question on Dr. King's essay might be as follows:

> In this letter, how does Dr. King establish the morality of his nonviolent campaign?

Since King used implicit methods (e.g., patriotic and religious allusions) to establish his campaign's moral authority, answering this second question requires an understanding of how King employed these methods to address criticism of his actions. The question asks for both an understanding of King's ideas and his methods of expressing them.

The third level of comprehension, the *experiential* level, involves a personal understanding or application of the material, an understanding which relates the text to a person's own experience and knowledge, or relates concepts from the text to other situations. It is at this deepest level that a book or an article becomes meaningful to a student, becomes a vehicle of new insight and discovery. One might pose the following experiential-level question about King's essay to students:

> Are Dr. King's philosophy and methods applicable to any social problems facing us today? If so, in what ways?

Whatever level of comprehension you are requiring of your students, you can use writing to help students achieve that comprehension. The act of writing out an answer to a text-explicit question helps to strengthen one's memory of the material. Writing a response to an experiential-level question helps one connect deeply to a text and understand its significance.

IMPROVING READING COMPREHENSION

Here are five techniques you can use to improve your students' reading:

1. Anticipation guides

2. Selective reading guides

3. Graphic organizers

4. Vocabulary previews

5. Student journals

Each technique is flexible enough to adapt to almost any class; you may find that a combination of techniques will help your students profit the most from the time they spend reading.

Anticipation Guides

Since students' success on examinations and writing assignments usually depends on their ability to understand required readings, you may have already discovered problems with assignments such as the following:

> For tomorrow, read pages 56–74 in your text.

This assignment works only for highly motivated students who are strong readers and who are interested in the text. With little direction, most students often miss key ideas or issues which you see as central in the text . . . that is, if they read the assignment at all. Too often such unfocused assignments generate so little interest in the text that the students choose to do something else instead of read for the course.

An "anticipation guide" (Readence, Bean, and Baldwin, 1981, pp. 131–133) can help to solve this problem by calling attention to ideas you see as important in the readings and by stimulating a genuine interest in the assigned material. The guide looks like a quiz. It consists of a series of statements or questions related to the readings and requires students to choose from among the various responses the one they think is right. The students always do this *before* reading the required material.

What follows is a sample anticipation guide developed by an English instructor for students he was training as writing tutors; he handed it out in his class before the students read the second chapter of Mina Shaughnessy's *Errors and Expectations* (1977), a text on the teaching of basic writing.

Anticipation Guide for Chapter 2:
"Handwriting and Punctuation"

1. According to one estimate, the average high school student in England writes about:
   a. 1000 words per week
   b. 250 words per week
   c. 500 words per month
2. According to the same estimate, the average basic writing student in an American high school is likely to write about:
   a. 100 words per week
   b. 350 words per semester
   c. 250 words per month
3. Because poor handwriting is mainly caused by problems of muscle coordination, people who have this problem will be unable to overcome it by the time they reach young adulthood.

    Agree _____   Disagree _____
4. People who have to labor over the mechanical processes of writing are unable to use writing effectively as a thinking process.

    Agree _____   Disagree _____
5. The best way for a tutor to help a person with handwriting problems is to overlook the problem and focus on the content of the ideas themselves.

    Agree _____   Disagree _____

Anticipation guides don't take long at all to fill out—five or ten minutes at most—and you can have the students respond to them in class or at home before they begin to read the assignment. Some instructors, by having the students fill out the guides in class, find them to be excellent starting points for class discussions. One psychology professor has his students complete a guide before viewing instructional films; he discovered that the guides significantly increase the students' interest in the films and help them focus on important points. (The correct responses to statements 1 and 2, incidentally, are "a" and "b" respectively; 3 and 5 are false, and 4 is true.)

Selective Reading Guides

Another instructional tool that will increase your students' comprehension and interest is a selective reading guide. Developed by Cunningham and Shablak, who referred to the device as a "Selective Reading Guide-O-Rama" (1975), it consists of a series of statements which guide students through the reading of a specific text and which highlight the most significant information in the text. Cal Poly instructor Richard L. Johnson wrote a guide to help his American Civilization students understand the key concepts presented in Rufus Miles' *Awakening from the American Dream* (1976), a book on which he asked his students to write a critique:

Selective Reading Guide

pp.

1–5   Read these pages carefully, for they explain the main ideas and approaches used in the book. After reading these pages, write down at least four questions which show your desire for more detailed explanation and information regarding several of the author's main points.

223–36 Now read this summary statement. You now know the main points of the book after only 20 minutes. You can now read faster with less danger of missing important points.

7–20   This chapter explains the graph on p. 10 and raises key questions. How convincing do you find the graphed information? What else do you want to know?

21–44   What caused our affluence? Of the many factors listed, select the three most important. Are they renewable or non-renewable? Moore, ch. 3, ties American identity to a frontier mentality. What does this chapter imply about our national identity?

41–61   Focus here on 58–61, the key question of jobs. Do you find the argument convincing? Explain.

62–75   First read the summary on 74–75. Key ideas are on 63, 71, 74. On p. 71 Miles outlines his idea of political limits, an important contribution on which he elaborates in Ch. 11.

76–88   The argument of perceived "rights" exceeding responsibilities can be easily grasped. Skim 76–84. But *note closely* the impact this has on the disintegration of community, pp. 85–88. Do you agree with the analysis? What implications are there for our own actions, both individually and in groups?

89–99   Draw a picture illustrating the chapter title. To me, this is a dynamite chapter. What does Miles see as the effect of high energy usage upon the family? the community? Does it have to be that way? Is energy usage the real "villain"? Look at Cal Poly's parking lot and read the section indicting the automobile, 95–99. Do you still love your car?

99–101 The "commons" idea is very important. Draw a series of pictures to explain it.

101–03   In the five years since this was written, what has occurred either to support or to deny Miles' hope?

104–20   Skip this if you already know it.

121–35   Most of this is familiar too, but note the fresh argument on 122–23. Miles' alternative is solar energy, which he feels encourages democracy. Is this Jefferson all over again? Evaluate 134–35 in terms of the Hamiltonian concern for a strong national defense. Would Hamilton agree that solar energy was a viable alternative? Why or why not?

136–51   Skip this. You should know it already.

152–69   Now the hard question: What must be done? What are the alternatives suggested by Miles? Can you add others? Which alternative do you choose? How will your alternative affect America? How will it affect the world?

170–90   Here is the major new contribution this book offers. Consider it carefully. Note your reasons for agreement or disagreement with Miles. Come to class prepared to defend a specific viewpoint.

191–207 The main point is on 204–07. The rest I suspect you know already and can skip. But have you considered before the problems raised on 204–07? What is your response?

208–19   Define "problematique." The ethical dimensions are extremely difficult. Consider our present traditions. What will we have to discard? What new ethics will we have to create? As one example, must we *encourage* abortion in our society? Lots of luck grappling with these. Try to *identify* ethical choices even if you cannot say where you stand on them.

220–22   Simply put, what do you make of this strange argument?

The selective reading guides can be powerful instructional tools. In Johnson's American Civilization class that did not have a guide, students reported that Miles' book was of little or no value to them. When Johnson introduced the selective reading guide in a subsequent class, he found that his students not only understood the text better, but that written reports improved as well. What most impressed him was the change in attitude toward the book (a text on the impact of declining resources on the American dream): over 90% of the students in the later class found the text highly valuable.

Graphic Organizers

It isn't always necessary to have students analyze their readings through a verbal medium only. Pictures and diagrams can help too. One special kind of diagram, a graphic organizer (Earle and Barron, 1969), has been shown to improve students' understanding of a text. As an example of this helpful device, here is an organizer of the first chapter of this book:

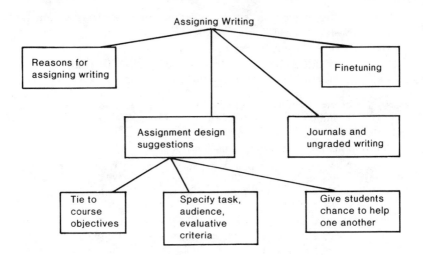

As you can see, the graphic organizer is a visual outline, a schematic diagram of a verbal text. It has the advantages of a conventional outline (with the additional clarity that graphic symbols can provide).

You can introduce the graphic organizer without having to expend a great deal of time; the time you do invest in it can substantially help your students improve their understanding of a text. At the end of one class session, for example, you can hand out a dittoed copy of a graphic organizer of their next reading assignment and explain how the students can make their own organizers of subsequent chapters. Or you can give your students incomplete organizers of upcoming chapters and have them fill in the blanks on their own.

Once your students have mastered this technique, they'll be able to represent pictorially the organization of each chapter or article they choose to diagram. Making an organizer takes a few minutes at most and promotes increased understanding and retention of what is read.

Vocabulary Previews

One of the most important tasks facing a student of any discipline is the mastery of that field's specialized vocabulary. For example, Readence, Bean, and Baldwin describe a student who understands that the outcome of a multiplication process remains the same no matter what the order of numbers may be, but who has difficulty comprehending a text that uses the term "commutative principle" (1981, pp. 105–106). The vocabulary preview, a relatively simple method you can use in your classes, can significantly improve your students' comprehension of their reading material. The method described below has been adapted from the "Preview in Context" developed by Readence, Bean, and Baldwin (1981, pp. 113–114).

To develop a preview you can look over an upcoming reading assignment and select key terms. You can present the words in written or oral form, doing so in the context of complete sentences. If, for example, you wanted your students to understand the concept of a "paradigm" (i.e., in the sense that Thomas Kuhn uses it in *The Structure of Scientific Revolutions*), you might present the following sentence to your students and ask them to infer the meaning of the word from its context:

> Galileo's discoveries completely changed our paradigm of the universe; no longer did we view the earth as the center.

If students had difficulty inferring the meaning of the word from a single example, additional sentences could help them understand the term.

The vocabulary preview need not take much time, yet it can be a powerful device for helping students unravel the meaning of complex material, and, like the anticipation guide, it can arouse their interest in the material as well.

Student Journals

The last technique helps students improve their reading comprehension and their writing fluency at the same time. This assignment requires that students keep a journal in which they write about what they are reading (textbook chapters, articles from professional journals, etc.). In Chapter I we described journals and other ungraded writing assignments; a journal in which students summarize or comment on readings is one of the most useful because it requires an active, critical response. Students who keep reading journals can better remember and understand the books and articles you assign.

Because most students have never written such a journal, it would be best to guide their writing, especially at the start of the course, with some general questions or topics that could be applied to anything they are reading. One reading journal format requires students to summarize briefly what they read and then respond to the text experientially. The following sample displays such a format:

Author: _____   Entry No. _____

Title: _____

Pages: _____

> Summary (Write from memory, noting what you recall as the main ideas of the selection):
>
> Connections and Applications: Write briefly on what the text means to you (e.g., do you agree or disagree? What are the implications of the ideas covered?). Then create an essay question about the text, a question that requires critical thinking (e.g., comparing, defining, analyzing). If time permits, answer the question.

Note that the "Connections and Applications" section encourages the students to synthesize lecture and textual material, and it suggests that they look ahead to questions they could encounter on their midterm or final examinations. Both tasks promote reading for meaning, for understanding, for insight. This is only one way of assigning a journal; however you choose to structure it, you'll be giving your students ways to process new information and make it their own.

VI
Evaluating Students' Writing

Evaluating students' writing poses a number of challenges. How can you give each paper adequate attention when you're faced with a large stack of papers and a limited amount of time? What comments will best help your students to improve their writing and their understanding of the subject matter? How extensively should you mark each paper? On what basis should you score or grade the papers? In this chapter we will present some answers to these and other questions.

THREE PHASES OF EVALUATION

A useful starting-point for evaluating students' writing is to separate the process into three phases: pre-evaluation, evaluation, and post-evaluation. Doing so will help you view the process systematically and look at each phase with specific questions in mind:

PRE-EVALUATION

1. How much time do I have for marking the whole batch? For each paper?
2. What objectives am I trying to fulfill in marking this particular set of papers?

EVALUATION

3. What aspects of each paper should I be marking?
4. What kinds of marks and comments would be most helpful to my students? How can I write those comments most efficiently?
5. How do I set appropriate grading standards?

POST-EVALUATION

6. What can I do when I return papers to point my students in the right direction?
7. How can I assist students whose writing reveals severe problems of development, organization, or mechanics?

Pre-Evaluation

Reviewing the objectives of a particular assignment before you mark your students' papers can often save you considerable time. A book critique that calls primarily for a basic understanding of a text will demand a different kind of feedback than a research paper that requires independent thinking and the synthesizing of ideas. By reviewing in advance your assignment's objectives and your evaluative criteria, you'll be able to focus your comments on the most important areas of the writing task. If possible, write an essay in which you yourself respond to the assignment. Doing so can deepen your understanding of the task you gave your students; it can also reveal problems in the wording or structure of the assignment.

Evaluation

Evaluating papers, like writing them, can be extremely time-consuming and wearing on one's nerves and spirit. Like writing, however, it can be approached systematically—as a process. Though your own method may differ from the process we offer below, we present it for two reasons: to offer a sequence that has worked well for a number of instructors, and to stimulate a consideration for the way you go about marking and scoring. Here, then, are steps you can take:

1. *Read through the batch quickly, sorting according to a specific formula:* Don't spend too much time doing this; the idea is to get a quick overview of the range of papers and of the kinds of problems you'll encounter in the writing. As you read, sort according to a formula that suits you best; some instructors sort the papers into stacks of good, fair, and poor essays. Others sort the papers by degrees of legibility. A few faculty find it helpful to read the worst papers first, saving the better pieces for "dessert" and motivating themselves to go on. Others prefer to read the best papers at the beginning, helping them set standards in their minds as they read and preparing them to recognize the shortcomings of the weaker papers as they appear in the stack.

Whichever method you use, sorting can give you a much needed overview of the material and help to structure your reading as you go along.

2. *Read each paper twice, first to identify its general weaknesses and strengths and then to pinpoint specific problems:* The first reading is an overview. It will give you a general sense of the writer's argument, and in many poorly organized papers, it will give you a picture of the writer's direction, a direction not always apparent at the beginning of the paper.

After you have surveyed the paper, go back, making notes in the margins and raising questions where the meaning is unclear (see "What and How to Mark"). After completing this closer textual reading, you'll be able to make at the end of the paper the general comments that summarize your overall impression and your suggestions for improvement. Then you'll be ready to score or grade the paper.

3. *After marking and grading all the papers, review each paper's grade, making appropriate adjustments whenever necessary:* Once you have finished grading the papers, you will have encountered a full range of responses, allowing you to make sharper distinctions in grades than you may have made at the beginning of the process. Knowing these distinctions can help you revise grades as you see fit; papers that may not have particularly high marks on the first reading through may now reveal themselves to be among the better responses to the assignment. On the other hand, papers which seemed to be outstanding at first may pale in comparison to even better writing you come across later in the batch. We are not suggesting that you use or avoid a curve in grading, only that you allow some flexibility to account for the overall performance of all your students on a particular assignment.

What to Mark? How Much to Mark?

The most time-consuming part of the evaluation process is the actual marking of papers. After all, it is a writing process which in itself entails difficult decisions about how and what to communicate to your students. You'll want the time you spend to be worthwhile; you'll want the comments you've labored over to have an effect—and certainly not to be ignored by the student writers you are helping. What, then, can you do to make the effort you expend result in a much improved learning experience for the students?

At the outset it is helpful to realize that the marking process begins even before you pick up a pen or marking pencil. As you read a paper through on the first time around, you'll be surveying it with a number of questions in your mind. By keeping those questions focused on large substantive and organization issues, you'll be able to look beyond the features of this or that sentence. Here are five major questions to consider in your first reading of the paper:

1. Is the writer addressing all parts of the assignment fully?

2. Is the main idea clear?

3. Is the main idea adequately developed and explained?

4. Are there logical connections among the various parts of the argument?

5. Does the writer show an adequate understanding of technical or specialized vocabulary and concepts?

Viewing a paper with these larger concepts in mind can make the writing of marginal comments on the second reading easier; you'll be able to point out problems and strengths with an understanding of how each section of the paper relates to the whole.

Writing Marginal Notes

The marginal notes you write can help you address large issues while still referring to specific parts of the text; here are some suggestions for writing effective marginal comments:

1. *Stress the positive:* You may recall from your own experience as a student the encouragement and motivation you derived from instructors who took the time to acknowledge good work, good ideas, good expression. Unfortunately, it is easy to forget this experience and concentrate instead on the weaknesses or flaws in a student's paper. A simple comment, however, such as "Good point!" or "well-expressed" shows your awareness of the student's effort and can often inspire greater achievement on the next assignment.

2. *Focus your comments:* Just as you look for unity in your students' writing, so too do they deserve some unity in the comments you make on their papers. In other words, your communication to them will carry far more weight if you emphasize major problems and strengths instead of diffusing your marks over every problem you can find. A few well-chosen questions ("How does this connect to your main idea?" "How might you develop this assertion?") can often do far more to stimulate your students' awareness of their writing than voluminous commentary. In short, the clarity of your own comments and questions will demonstrate eloquently to students your concern for clear and concise expression on their part.

3. *Mark grammatical problems only if they significantly obscure the meaning:* Students who have major grammatical or mechanical problems usually gain little benefit from the correction or marking of all the errors in their papers. Therefore, when you find that the errors significantly hinder your understanding, significantly interrupt the flow of reading, you need not burden yourself with the painstaking marking of all the errors. You can be more effective by marking just one or two examples of the most egregious errors, or by commenting at the end of the paper about the mechanical problems. Your efforts will indicate that an instructor other than an English teacher has pinpointed mechanical errors as a barrier to communication—and also as a barrier (sometimes hidden, sometimes not) to a students' academic success.

One more note about the marking of mechanical problems: since you need not correct them, you also do not need to master the vocabulary of error. You need not know the mysteries of dangling modifiers or fused sentences in order to get a message across to students. A simple injunction ("The mechanical errors here disrupt the reading of your paper; I recommend that you get help with them at the Learning Center.") will suffice.

Writing Summary Comments

The summary comments you write at the end of a paper allow you to address the most important strengths and weaknesses in the writing. If a student's major problem is the lack of a clear thesis, the summary comments can be an excellent means of pointing out the problem and suggesting an improvement on a revision or on the next assignment. Problems with logic, development, or vocabulary can be similarly addressed. Whatever the difficulties or strengths of the paper may be, the summary notes help crystallize your evaluation and focus your recommendations. When written well, they give the students a strong foundation for improvement.

Some Ways of Marking

Specific examples can better represent the ideas we have discussed than lengthy explanations; the two examples that follow represent the kind of focused feedback that instructors can give to their students. Both themes were written on an impromptu basis in response to the following question:

> Most people have read a book or seen a play, movie, or television program that has affected their feelings or behavior in some important way. Discuss such an experience of your own. (1) Describe the book, play, movie, or television program that affected you. (2) Tell how it affected you and (3) explain why you regard it as important.

This topic was developed for the English Placement Test used in the California State University system; the students wrote the papers under test conditions and had only forty-five minutes to plan and write their essays. For clarity we have presented the essays in typed form, and we have marked the papers to illustrate the kinds of focused comments that would help students to rewrite.

THE DEERHUNTER

With the Academy Awards over now, we are all probably
quite familiar with the name "Deerhunter". I myself
viewed this film a few evenings ago and was caught up in *Word choice):*
Look this up.
its gripping story from the first moment. Militaristic
plots have always been fascinating to me and this film
strengthened my interest like no other film I have seen
apostrophe
before. The key reason for this being the films incredibly *sentence*
fragment
accurate real life situations of death and horror as seen
in the Vietnam War. *Describe briefly. Your reader may*
not have seen the movie!

It is amazing how a film can bring to life all the
What fears? Whose? *What incidents?*
fears, cruelty, and true to life <u>incidents</u>. For someone

to write such a film, one would think he actually had to

live through it to picture all these horrors. This film
Describe one or two.
captures <u>moments</u> that sane poeple only dream about and

ponder with extreme fear. Their natural instinct is to

shut it out. But what of the prisoners who actually *Does the movie*

lived that nightmare? They couldn't turn off the *depict events*

television set or leave the room. What they were *that actually took place?*

experiencing was cold, hard, solid, and unescapable.

At times I'm sure they thought it must all be just a

dream. Then they would suddenly come back to earth and

realize what was transpiring.

It really shocked me to see such inhumanity when

all I'm used to is crime-drama television programs. I

mean, who'd ever believe that such a world could ever

exist where people mutilate and destroy one another. And
for what? *Did the movie affect you in any other way, in addition to shocking you?*

The fact that war is hanging over the heads of all

Americans at present truly shocks me after having seen

this movie. This fact, I believe, is the main reason

the movie affected me so. It was as though I might be

the one who is being tortured or killed. I will be the

one losing my mind because of overwhelming circumstances.

And I for one cannot picture myself in this situation.

Hopefully no one will have to live out these horrors as
who?
<u>they</u> did in the film, for I'm sure that the real life

pains hurt much more than watching them being inflicted

upon others.
This essay shows your reaction to the film but does not make clear what shocked you—even to a reader who has seen the movie. Describe the movie briefly (plot, characters, setting).

Also, this essay could speak more directly to the third point: Why is the movie important? What's the significance of the shock or horror? What does the movie show about war? About human nature?

40

No story, comical or dramatic, has affected me more
than the series M*A*S*H which looks at life, it situations ✗
and its lessons, during a war. War always seems to teach
a person something about life, but it is also war which
changes it. [In]MASH[it is made easier to understand]the   *shows*
traumas which take place before and after [a]war[-type   *during?*
experience.]   [ ] =omit :
                Cut unnecessary phrases.

The setting for a war story always seems to center   *Describe the*
around a battleground; in MASH this is not so. The   *setting briefly:*
                                agreement   *which war?*
battleground and all its glorious aura is brought into   *What is a*
                                          SP   *MASH*
the operating rooms and emergency wards. The affects of   *unit?*
agreement : effects .... are
war is what MASH is out to show and it is that which

gives persons like myself a new understanding about the
                    punctuation
abruptness of life - When the soldiers, not even graduates
from high school, are brought in with devastating wounds
no such word
a stunness comes about. The harshness of war can not
                    What is a straight forward scene?
always be understood in such straight forward scenes, *punctuation*
I'm not sure what you mean here.
there must be a mixture of humanity coming in and it is
provided by the looniest of characters.

                                                who are the
In MASH there are the All-American boys, the heart   *heart*
                                                     seekers?
seekers, the panty watchers, the old soldiers, the funny
          (what are the rest on your list?)
men, and most of all human beings. Heading the camp
                    word choice
hospital is an old but fruitful colonel who shows all
not clear what you mean here
feelings in the brightest of light. Taking care of him
Radar (Use characters' names!)
is the innocent post-adolescent corporal who also serves
  ^
as the company clerk. Through the harsh realities he
                    word choice | I find this
sees throughout the hospital his tenderness is compacted *confusing.*
and he must do his duties. Adding comical light are the
two captain doctors who besides surgery find time to
          word choice
chase the women and shoot a few rounds of golf a day.
These two men with all their hilarious antics dole out

41

word show *punctuation*

the most pr<u>evious</u> of human emotions, love. Love ~~to~~ *for* ⎫ *sentence*
their work and the people whom they try to save day ⎭ *fragment*

after day, hour after hour. Their loyalty to life makes

for?
me think twice about what I'm doing <u>to</u> other people.

Military stories always talk about life, but not in

the spectacular fashion which "MASH" does. What must be *Describe*

shown to the viewers are the realities of war and what it *elements*
can you give an example or two? *of MASH*
does to people both physically and mentally. Sure, the *that make*
What lessons? *it so*
blood and horror affect me but it is the <u>lessons</u> learned *spectacular.*

which stay with me. It is why the people are there that

affects me. It is why all the horror of war happens *This paragraph*

which affects me. It is the humanity poured out of *repeats what*
you've already
every finger in that place which affects me the most. *said.*

The show MASH has been able to bring me to a new

understanding about life, its pleasures and its horrors.

Life is taught on that screen, more than any book or *overstated?*

motion picture could explain. It is with all the heroism ⎫ *I'm not*
⎪ *sure what*
and comical incidents that the life on that screen can be ⎬ *you mean*
⎪ *here.*
transferred into my soul. Life, it takes a funny show ⎭
unclear
with a serious situation <u>which explains it all</u>.

*This essay addresses all aspects of the question,
although one or two examples of events depicted in
the series would add to your description of the
show and also support and clarify your
comments about its importance. Most of your
description focuses on characters.*

*You have structured this essay with a
clear beginning, middle, and end. The impact
of your paper is weakened, however, by problems
with vague phrasing and word choice.*

SCORES AND SCORING GUIDES

Giving grades can often be as difficult as receiving them. Setting standards is usually a complex matter, involving a host of criteria which may be difficult to weigh. Two systems can help you overcome this difficulty: scoring guides and analytic scales. Both of these help to stabilize the criteria for student and instructor alike, making the process considerably more objective than otherwise.

Scoring guides contain descriptions of papers meriting different numerical or letter grades. One such guide is used to evaluate impromptu essays written as part of the Graduation Writing Test at Cal Poly Pomona:

Possible Scores

6   A superior response will address itself to all aspects of the question. Through it may have occasional faults, it will be well organized, detailed, and generally well written.

5–4   These scores will be useful for a well-handled paper that is weak in some aspects of the superior response; e.g., it may slight one of the parts of the question; it may not be as clearly organized as the superior response; it may have some minor grammatical inconsistencies. Otherwise, the paper should be competently written.

3   This score will be useful for the following kinds of papers:
—those that are only descriptive or narrative
—those in which the language is overly cliched
—those that are overly repetitious
—those that are general and superficial

This score will also be useful for papers that are developed with some specificity and detail but are marred by more than a few minor grammatical inconsistencies.

2   This score is to be used for papers that exhibit serious weaknesses in structure, syntax, diction and/or development.

1   This score is to be used for papers that show very little understanding of the question or suggest incompetence in structure, syntax, and diction.

Such guides are used extensively in the scoring of essays written for entrance and proficiency tests. When large numbers of readers are assembled to read and rank the essays, scoring guides provide the basis for a common set of standards, making it possible for different readers to come to reasonably close agreement in scoring. When using such guides in your own classes, you can attach them to your syllabus, letting students know at the outset the criteria and standards you'll use to rate their papers. The guides give students a clear sense of what to strive for; in addition, the numerical scores do not carry the same connotations that letter grades do. The numbers are simply correspondences with specific descriptions, and the students can quickly understand from the guides the kind of goals they should be striving for.

Dichotomous and analytic scales, on the other hand, permit you to identify specific strengths and weaknesses in the writing. They involve series of sub-scores devoted to areas you deem important in the students' writing. Here are two such scales, a dichotomous scale employing "yes" or "no" questions related to specific features of the writing, and an analytic scale that employs a range of numerical scores.

DICHOTOMOUS SCALE FOR EVALUATING WRITING

	YES	NO	
SUBSTANCE	____	____	1. Paper addresses the issue.
	____	____	2. Paper has a focus, central idea.
	____	____	3. Paper develops major aspects of the central idea.
	____	____	4. Paper shows awareness of importance of main ideas.
ORGANIZATION	____	____	5. Structure or pattern of the paper is clear.
	____	____	6. Paper has an introduction, development and conclusion.
	____	____	7. Each paragraph is coherent.
	____	____	8. Transitions from one idea to next are logical.
MECHANICS	____	____	9. Sentence structure is correct.
	____	____	10. Sentences are not awkward.
	____	____	11. Sentences are varied.
	____	____	12. Errors in use of verbs are few.
	____	____	13. Errors in use of pronouns are few.
	____	____	14. Errors in use of modifiers are few.
	____	____	15. Errors in word usage are few.
	____	____	16. Punctuation errors are few.
	____	____	17. Spelling errors are few.

	YES	NO	
EVIDENCE	____	____	18. Statements are accurate.
	____	____	19. Opinions are adequately supported.
	____	____	20. Sources are identified and documented appropriately.
MECHANICS (alternative)	____	____	Paper shows control of grammar.
	____	____	Paper shows control of syntax.
	____	____	Paper has few misspellings.

ANALYTIC SCALE FOR EVALUATING WRITING

I. SUBSTANCE

A. Focus	2	4	6	8	10
B. Development	2	4	6	8	10
C. Significance	2	4	6	8	10

II. ORGANIZATION

A. Structure	2	4	6	8	10
B. Coherence	2	4	6	8	10
C. Paragraphing	2	4	6	8	10

III. MECHANICS

A. Grammar	2	4	6	8	10
B. Sentence Structure	2	4	6	8	10
C. Spelling	2	4	6	8	10
D. Punctuation	2	4	6	8	10

IV. EVIDENCE

A. Accuracy	2	4	6	8	10
B. Support	2	4	6	8	10
C. Documentation	2	4	6	8	10

The vocabulary of these scales (*Substance, Organization, Mechanics, and Evidence*) was taken from the Student/Faculty Handbook on Writing Reinforcement (1981) developed at Cal State San Bernardino. If you use such scales, you may want to experiment with your own evaluative vocabulary, focusing on areas most important to the assignments you give.

Post-Evaluation: Returning the Papers

If you consider each part of the writing assignment as an opportunity for the student to grow and learn, then you can use the few minutes in which you hand back papers to underscore major ideas, major criteria for evaluation. In fact, that short time can often be the most significant moment of communication; it can be the time in which students are most alert, most interested in the reasons for the marks on their papers.

Probably the most useful thing you can do, aside from explaining how and why you marked the papers as you did, is to distribute sample papers that showed strengths in particular areas. Many instructors do this—and with great success. When receiving their marked papers, students are particularly keen to see the reasons for another's success. You can often derive the equivalent of hours of instruction from the handing out of a single good example; nothing speaks as clearly as an exemplary theme.

In addition to these efforts, many faculty encourage students to see them individually for additional explanations of the grade and the marks. We believe that this practice can be helpful to instructors as well as to students. Often you will never know how students will interpret your marks until they have asked you about them. Then, as many instructors have discovered, the students haven't understood the comments. Conferences can be a way of elaborating on written comments—and discovering what did and did not communicate to the students.

The Student with Special Problems

Occasionally you will have students whose garbled syntax, disorganized paragraphs, or severe mechanical problems may indicate substantial problems beyond the scope of your own immediate assistance. The way such cases can be handled will vary from class to class, college to college. In some situations the services of an outside tutor may be helpful (i.e., from a learning or tutorial center); in other cases you may recommend that the student take a remedial or basic writing course. But though the specific solution will depend on the student's situation, the most important step you can take is to notify the student of the problem at the earliest possible date. A paper assigned early in the term, a prompt response to it by the instructor, a timely conference with the student—all of these will ensure a realistic, sensible approach, will help preclude the panic and frustration that occur when the problem is recognized too late.

REFERENCES

Earle, R. A., and Barron, R. F. An Approach for Teaching Vocabulary in Content Subjects. In *Research in Reading in the Content Areas: Second Year Report*. Ed. H. L. Herber and R. F. Barron. Syracuse, N.Y.: Reading and Language Arts Center, Syracuse University, 1973, pp. 84–110.

Flower, Linda S. and Hayes, John R. "Problem-Solving Strategies and the Writing Process." *College English,* 39 (1977), 449–461.

Fulwiler, Toby E. "Journal Writing Across the Curriculum." In *How to Handle the Paper Load*. Ed. Gene Stanford and the Committee on Classroom Practices. Urbana, Ill.: National Council of Teachers of English, 1979, pp. 15–22.

Grobe, Shelly F., and Grobe, Cary H. "Reading Skills as a Correlate of Writing Ability in College Freshman." *Reading World,* (Oct. 1977), pp. 50–54.

Herrington, Anne J. "Writing to Learn: Writing Across the Disciplines." *College English,* 43 (1981), 379–387.

Lanham, Richard A. *Revising Prose*. New York: Charles Scribner's Sons, 1979.

Lunsford, Andrea A. "What We Know and Don't Know About Remedial Writing." *College Composition and Communication,* (Feb., 1978), pp. 47–51.

Miles, Rufus. *Awakening From the American Dream*. New York: Universe, 1976.

Readence, John E.; Bean, Thomas W.; and Baldwin, R. Scott. *Content Area Reading: An Integrated Approach*. Dubuque, Iowa: Kendall-Hunt. 1981.

Shaughnessy, Mina P. *Errors and Expectations*. New York: Oxford University Press, 1977.

Smith, Frank. *Understanding Reading, Second Edition*. New York: Holt, Rinehart, and Winston, 1978.

When Professionals Must Write:
A Selection of On-The-Job Writing Tasks

Though couched in general terms, the descriptions of writing and reading tasks that follow are based on actual interviews with professionals working in southern California firms and organizations. The assignments described are the particular tasks of the individuals interviewed and are not intended to represent the writing projects of all professionals in a given field.

1. BANK ADMINISTRATOR

    a. *Task:* To write a credit memorandum which would recommend that credit be extended or renewed to a corporation or business. Running roughly 35–40 pages (one-fourth of which will be text and the other three-fourths financial data), the memorandum may concern lines of credit ranging from $10 million to $100 million. Although writers will compose the memoranda on their own, it is recommended that they share drafts and discuss them with colleagues to allow for ideas to be checked and issues to be raised.

    b. *Audience and Purpose:* Bank management officials will read and decide upon the request. The writer's purpose must be to convince these officials to follow the course of action recommended in the memo.

    c. *Requirements:* The composing of this memorandum will require the writer to:

        (1) Plan and conduct thorough and accurate research into such factors as the company's history, profit and loss, and working capital.

        (2) Assemble the data in appropriate form.

        (3) Analyze the data to provide a concrete basis for decision making.

        (4) Synthesize the findings to develop a cogent, persuasive statement.

    d. *Evaluative Criteria:* The memorandum will be evaluated with these criteria in mind:

        (1) Was the necessary financial data researched accurately and thoroughly?

        (2) Did the recommendations of the memo follow logically from the data presented?

        (3) Was the writing coherent and concise? Could a reader clearly follow the transition from one point to another?

        (4) Was the writing free of spelling, usage, and punctuation errors? Such errors undermine the writer's stature in the mind of the reader.

e. *Other Writing Tasks:*

   (1) Proposals (for equipment, staff, money, or other resources). Such proposals are often written by branch managers and other operations personnel.

   (2) Performance evaluations of employees.

   (3) Letters (to customers as well as to bank administration officials). These include letters of complaint as well.

2. PROGRAMMER OR ENGINEER IN A COMPUTER COMPANY

   a. *Task:* To write, in collaboration with other programmers or engineers, any one of a number of documents (or sections of documents) related to the development of a computer or computer system. The document may be any of the following:

   (1) An initial project definition (describing the computer or system to be built).

   (2) Functional specifications (describing the capacities of the product).

   (3) Design specifications (describing the product's specific technical dimensions).

   (4) User documentation (technical manuals to be used by customers).

The writing of all the documents related to a specific product may take from a few months to over a year to complete. The individual programmer working on a project may work in teams of from four to six people, writing sections of a manuscript and submitting them to peer review in team meetings set at various intervals. It is important to note that although various documents connected to a specific product may be distinct from one another, their development is part of a single, unified process.

   b. *Audience and Purpose:* The audiences will vary from document to document. Some texts (e.g., the initial project definition) may be read by company management or potential clients, while others (e.g., the design specifications) are intended for technical staff within the company. The purposes of the documents may range from persuasion (e.g., convincing a reader of a project's merits) to explanation (e.g., describing the components of a system and their interrelations).

   c. *Requirements:* Although the special requirements will vary from document to document, the writing of any of the texts may require an engineer or programmer to:

   (1) Explain technical concepts in language readable by other specialists, or, in a number of cases, by non-technical readers.

    (2) Collaborate with other professionals and be willing to take criticism of one's writing by colleagues.

  d. *Evaluative Criteria:* The writing will be evaluated with these questions in mind:

    (1) Are the explanations and descriptions clearly organized? Or are there gaps in the explanations which hinder a reader's understanding?

    (2) Is the information technically correct and accurate?

    (3) Is the writing free from errors of syntax, usage, spelling, and punctuation? (This concern is less important than criteria #1 and #2.)

3. ARCHITECT (SMALL ARCHITECTURE AND PLANNING FIRM)

  a. *Task:* To write, in collaboration with a planner, a proposal for the development of a specific piece of land. The proposal will outline the structure and extent of development, whether it be of a shopping plaza, a housing tract, or a small neighborhood.

  b. *Audience and Purpose:* The audience will be a potential client (e.g., a land developer), and the purpose may be to secure a contract or complete a preliminary step in an already contracted project.

  c. *Requirements:* When putting together the proposal the writer may be asked to:

    (1) Help synthesize and explain various kinds of information (architectural, environmental, financial) related to the proposed development.

    (2) Work collaboratively with a planner.

    (3) Write (often) under severe time constraints.

  d. *Evaluative Criteria:* The proposal may be evaluated in the following terms:

    (1) Is it concise?

    (2) Is it accurate?

    (3) Is the style appropriate (i.e., does the tone of the writing convey the image which the firm seeks to project)?

    (4) Is the writing free of errors of spelling, usage, grammar, and punctuation? Such errors do affect the image which the writer may seek to convey.

e. *Other Writing Tasks:*

   (1) Marketing brochures and letters introducing the firm.

   (2) Planning feasibility studies.

   (3) Contracts.

   (4) Environmental impact reports.

   (5) Technical specifications for a project.

f. *Reading:* A Vital Tool

   (1) In order to command the language and concepts of proposals, environmental impact reports (EIR's), or other writing projects, the architect must be continually reading. The only way he or she will be able to write an EIR, for example, will be to survey the format and language used in other completed reports.

   (2) According to another architect (who works for a large, highly diversified firm), reading also provides a means by which a professional's ideas are continually challenged and kept vital. Through reading contemporary reviews, articles, and books, architects are given the opportunity to ask questions, to explore alternative approaches, and to view their work against the background of contemporary developments. One's ideas of what is fitting, tasteful, or beautiful are as much shaped by language as by direct encounters with a building project or an environment.

4. RESEARCH SCIENTIST AND ADMINISTRATOR

   a. *Task:* To write a grant proposal requesting funds for a research project.

   b. *Audience and Purpose:* The audience may be a grant-review committee of a governmental agency or private foundation. The purpose is to convince the committee of the merits of the project's goals and methods. As one scientist stated, "You can't get started (i.e., as a researcher) unless you can write."

   c. *Requirements:* The completion of such a task will require the writer to:

      (1) Gain as accurate a sense of the audience (the grant review committee) as possible.

      (2) Articulate research aims clearly and demonstrate logically how each method achieves the project's aims.

      (3) Anticipate potential questions and answer them in the text of the proposal.

      (4) Submit drafts for preliminary review by colleagues.

d. *Evaluative Criteria:*

    (1) Is the writing organized to build a case logically?

    (2) Is the project feasible? Can the researcher do what he or she has set out to do in the proposed period of time?

    (3) Does the writing concisely describe the aims and methods of the project without omitting explanations (particularly in the methods section)?

    (4) Has the writer attended to all the details of the proposal including spelling, usage, and punctuation? As one scientist declared, "If the proposal is sloppily written, there's some question raised about how seriously the writer wants the money."

e. *Other Tasks:* Part of a scientist's job is to write grant proposals; an equally important part is to describe the findings of various projects. "What other people see of your work," said one scientist, "is only what you can communicate about it."

    (1) Short, preliminary abstracts for meetings and conferences.

    (2) Short articles (4–6 pages).

    (3) Longer articles.

    (4) Monographs, chapters, and review articles (reviewing the state of the art in a particular field).

f. *The Role of Reading:* Because the volume of new scientific information is so great, up to one-fourth (or even more) of a scientist's time will be devoted to reading. In one area of brain research, for example, approximately thirty scientific journals bear directly on the field. A scientist must be able to sift through the mass of current information, abstract material most pertinent to his projects, and use the information appropriately.

5. ENGINEER (AEROSPACE/ELECTRONICS)

a. *Task:* To help write a section or sections of a proposal to construct a component or system (e.g., a radar system). The proposal will include technical, administrative, and financial sections, and may run to several hundred pages. Its production will be coordinated by company managers and the final text may represent the combined efforts of many teams of engineers (with the assistance, when necessary, of technical writing consultants and editors).

b. *Audience and Purpose:* In this particular case, the audience comprises officials of federal (defense) agencies who are considering alternative proposals from different companies. The agency solicits the proposals once it determines that a particular system is desired by the government.

The purpose of the proposal, therefore, will be to convince the agency that the company can deliver the best product in the most efficient and cost-effective manner possible. Although the writing is technical, its primary thrust is to persuade.

c. *Requirements:* As a member of a team working on a section of a proposal, an engineer must be able to:

   (1) Clearly identify the main concept which he or she wishes to convey about the particular sub-component in the design.

   (2) Articulate that main idea in a form as clear and as understandable as possible.

   (3) Organize the supporting material in such a fashion as to show clear links between the subtopics and the main idea.

   (4) Work collaboratively with peers in an ongoing review process.

d. *Evaluative Criteria:*

   (1) Does the writing develop a clear main concept? Are the descriptions concrete?

   (2) Is the language free from unnecessary jargon?

e. *Other Tasks:* These may include:

   (1) Internal proposals (i.e., those intended only for use within the company).

   (2) Design specifications for use within the company.

APPENDIX 2

Sample Accounting Assignment

The Students Are Given the Following Assignment
(developed by Cal Poly professors Alan Senn and Carol Holder)

Assume that you and a partner have an accounting firm. You have just accepted a new client, Gordon Blue, who has provided the following information during several conferences:

Blue is 58 years old and has a wife and three grown children. He has been the maitre d' at a prominent restaurant for twenty years and is now opening his own place.

Blue has posed several questions he wants you and your partner to answer:

1. What form of business enterprise should he set up for his new restaurant? What are the relative advantages and disadvantages of different forms?

2. Should he lease or buy the equipment? What are critical factors he should consider in making his decision?

3. What kinds of retirement plans are available for self-employed persons? He has heard about IRA and Keogh, but does not understand them.

4. Can and should he sell his home to raise capital needed in the business? He has heard that he can exclude profit of up to $100,000 in a sale of his residence.

5. Can he take a Nile cruise and claim some portion of the costs as business expenses as he plans to attend professional seminars en route? How might he make arrangements to legitimize deductions?

6. How can he give some of his wealth to his children effective at his death without creating for them a heavy tax liability?

7. How might he best take advantage of income averaging provisions of Federal tax law if his new business prospers as expected?

8. What does *internal control* of a business mean? What does it involve, for restaurants especially, and why is it important?

You and your partner have decided to take four questions apiece and draft responses for each question area. (You may prepare responses to **any** four of the questions.) In planning and writing these four reports, remember that Gordon Blue has little knowledge of accounting. He needs specific, concise responses written in non-technical language.

Students Meet in Small Groups

In addition to preparing written responses to four of the eight question areas, the students, working in teams, prepare to present an oral response to just one question. (The oral presentations will be made prior to the due date for the rough drafts of the written reports.)

On the day the teacher hands out the assignment, she divides the class into eight teams, assigning one question area to each team. These teams then meet to plan their presentation. In small group discussion, the students consider the question before them carefully, discuss what they know to be relevant advice, identify sub-questions that will need further research, plan their oral presentation, and divide among themselves the tasks of researching information and presenting the response.

Students Read, Write, Observe, etc.

On their own, the students work on their assignment from the small group, preparing to give an oral response to one area of one question. Also, students make preliminary decisions about the four questions for their written report.

Entire Group Responds to, Evaluates, Small Groups' Oral Reports

At the designated class meeting, each team gives, in an oral report, advice pertinent to one question area. The teacher and class act first as Gordon Blue, asking for clarification and raising further questions, and then as accounting experts, commenting on the accuracy and completeness of the advice.

Students (Individually) Research, Prepare, Write Rough Drafts; Instructor and Peers Evaluate Rough Drafts

Rough drafts are read aloud, projected, or exchanged so that students comment on and question each other's work; all receive some feedback from more than one person on what they've written. The advantage of using an opaque projector is that students can hear spontaneous reactions to their work from other students and from the instructor. All can learn simultaneously from each other's successes and shortcomings (even if there are few comments).

Students Write Final Drafts; Instructor and Peers Evaluate Final Drafts

Final drafts can be shared and evaluated as were the rough drafts. Following peer evaluation, the instructor comments on and grades the final drafts. These comments may be written, taped, or presented in a conference with the student. The comments should reflect the student's progress and suggest areas for improvement.

APPENDIX 3

Assigning Writing and Reading in the Disciplines: A Techniques Inventory

Assigning Writing

1. Focusing the writing task by clarifying instructions to the student.

2. Using groups to facilitate brainstorming and help students with early stages of writing the paper.

3. Using alternative audiences (e.g., fictitious audiences in "case" situations).

4. Improving essay exams by clarifying instructions and writing tasks (or adding essay or short-answer questions to exams that had none before).

5. Improving assignments or essay exams by articulating evaluative criteria to students.

6. Using journal or ungraded writing in or out of class.

7. Assigning an early paper for diagnostic purposes.

8. Assigning several short papers instead of one long one due at the end of the term.

9. Providing students with a model of a good student paper.

10. Requiring revision of weak papers.

11. Explaining desired format or structure of assigned paper.

Evaluating Writing

1. Using peer evaluation of papers (rough or final drafts).

2. Using holistic scoring.

3. Using a dichotomous or an analytic scale, a checklist or other grading system.

4. Focusing feedback in marginal and summary notes to the students.

5. Discussing papers in student-teacher conferences.

Assigning Reading

Using:

1. Anticipation guides.

2. Selective reading guides.

3. Graphic organizers.

4. Vocabulary previews.

5. Student journals.